SCHOLASTIC

BOB® BOOKS

Developing Readers Workbook

Long Vowels (K-1)

Ask for Bob Books® at your local bookstore, or visit www.bobbooks.com.

ISBN 978-93-5471-691-1

Printed in India

This reprint edition, August 2025

Bob Books: Long Vowels
Workbook

The Game

Read the story and color each picture. Then circle the words in each sentence that have a long "a" sound, as in "gate."

The Game

Kate was playing first base.
Dave threw the ball to Kate.

Jane made it to base.
Jane was safe on first base.

James hit the ball hard.

Kate got the ball.
She threw it to the base.

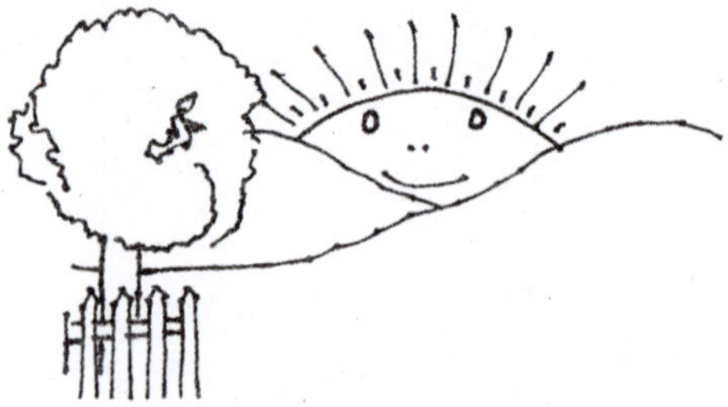

The ball game went on and on. The game went on until the sun set.

Say and write the words. Circle the letter that says its name, then cross out the silent letter.

game game

Jane

base

Kate

safe

gave

The Game

Circle and match the beginning letter to complete the correct word.

c b

K N

g w

-ave -ase -ate

J M

c s

g n

-afe -ame -ane

Circle the word that goes with the picture, then write the word on the line.

bat
base
clap

base

Jane
van
clam

cap
Kate
jar

Kate
safe
made

fan
gave
make

game
mat
ham

The Game

Read each sentence. Find the word that is wrong and write it in the red box. Write the correct word in the orange box.

Jane was save on first base.

save → safe

The ball gam went on and on.

→

Jane took the ball and bate.

→

She threw it to the bake.

→

Make complete sentences using the words from the box.

had Jane bat ball

______ ______ a ______

and ______ .

hit James ball

______ ______ the ______ .

home Jane went

______ ______ ______ .

The Game

Read each sentence, then draw a line to the correct picture.

Kate got the ball. She threw it to the base.

Jane made it to the base. Jane was safe on first base.

Jane took the ball and bat. Jane went home.

Kate was playing first base. Dave threw the ball to Kate.

Jake threw the ball over the plate. James hit the ball hard.

Look at each picture and fill in the missing vowel for each word.

c a t 

c a k e 

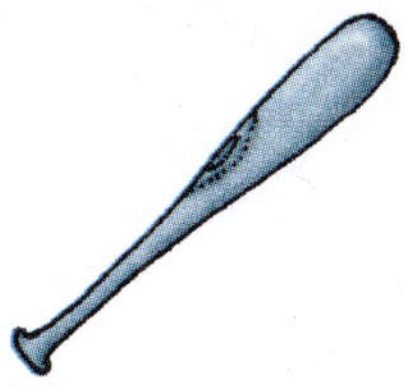

b ___ t

b ___ s ___

g ___ m ___

h ___ t

f ___ st

pl ___ n ___

Joe's Toe

Read the story and color each picture. Then circle the words in each sentence that have a long "o" sound, as in "home."

Joe's Toe

Joe rode his bike over a bump.

The bike hit a stone. Joe lost control of the bike.

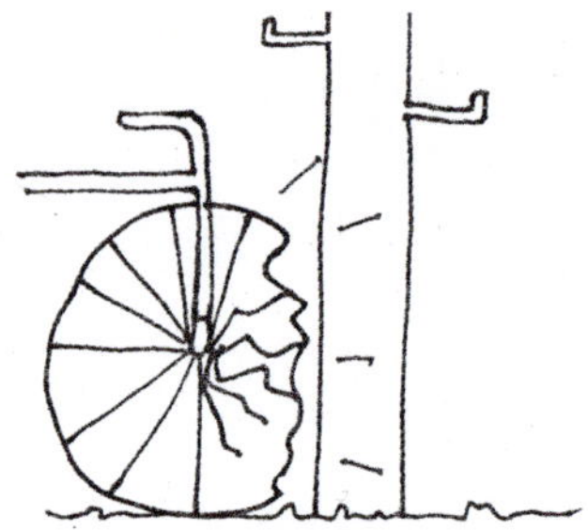

It bumped into a pole. Poor Joe had a jolt!

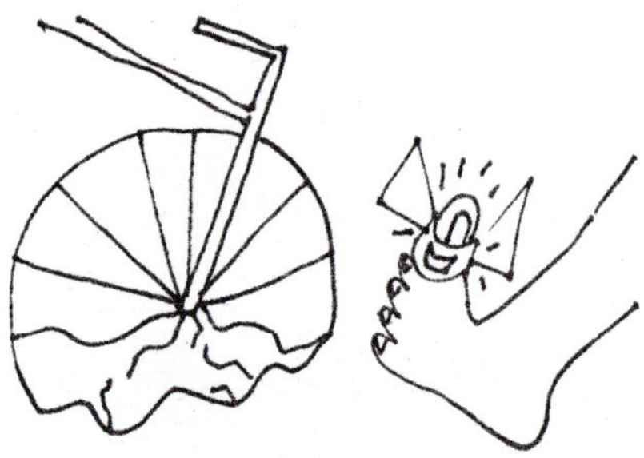

He broke his bike. He broke his big toe.

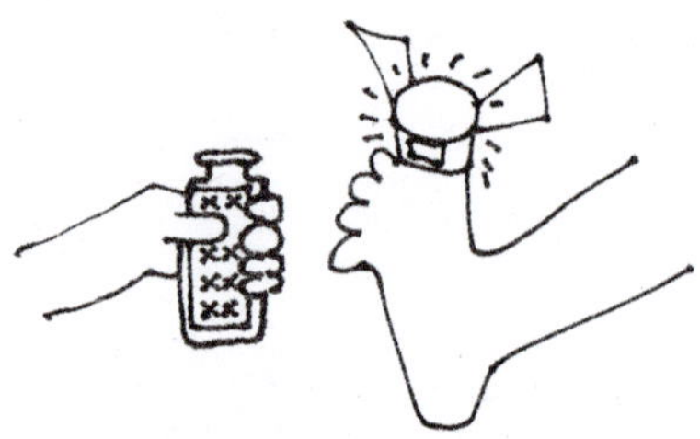

Sam took Joe to the doctor. The doctor fixed the broken toe.

Say and write the words. Circle the letter that says its name, then cross out the silent letter.

home home

stone

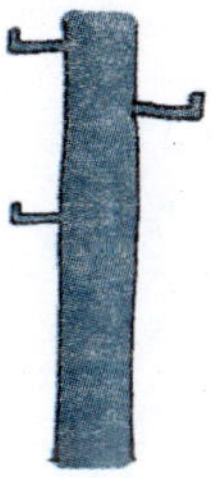

pole

Joe

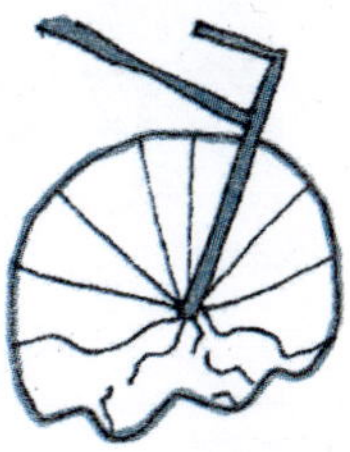

broke

toe

Joe's Toe

Circle and match the beginning letter to complete the correct word.

M J

d h

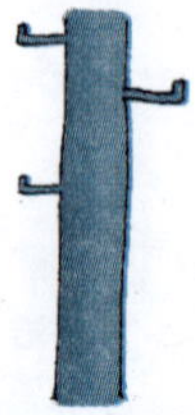

p m

-ome

-ole

-oe

c st

t m

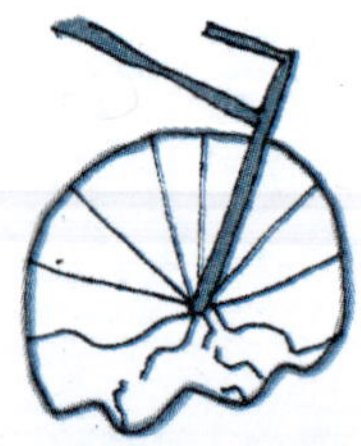

br sm

-one

-oke

-oe

Circle the word that goes with the picture, then write the word on the line.

top
home
frog

home

stone
pop
shop

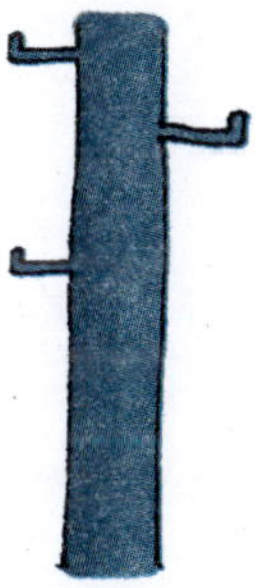

pot
pole
flop

doe
goes
Joe

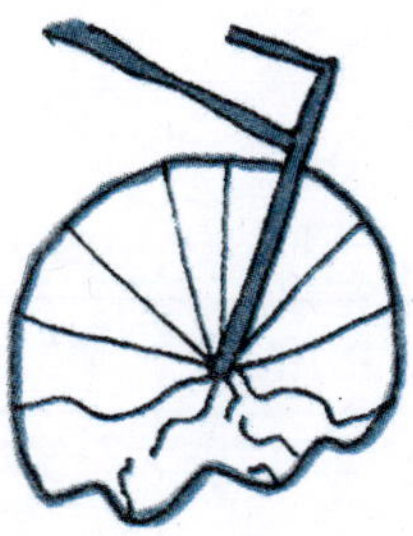

stone
broke
pole

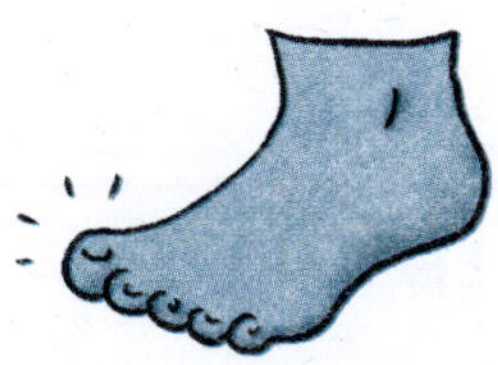

tea
toe
tree

Joe's Toe

Read each sentence. Find the word that is wrong and write it in the red box. Write the correct word in the orange box.

Sam and Joe went hope.

He broke his big Joe.

The bike hit a stop.

It bumped into a hole.

Make complete sentences using the words from the box.

his broke He bike

____ ____ ____ ____.

hit bike stone

The ____ ____ a ____.

good found tool Sam

____ ____ a ____ ____.

Joe's Toe

Read each sentence, then draw a line to the correct picture.

Joe rode his bike over a bump. ● ● 

He went head over heels. ● ● 

He broke his big toe. ● ● 

The doctor fixed the broken toe. ● ● 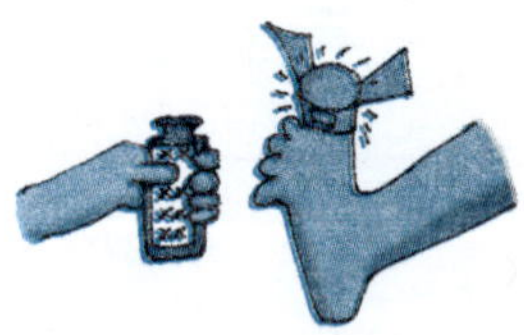

Sam fixed the broken bike. ● ● 

Look at each picture and fill in the missing vowel for each word.

b o x 

h o u se 

t o e 

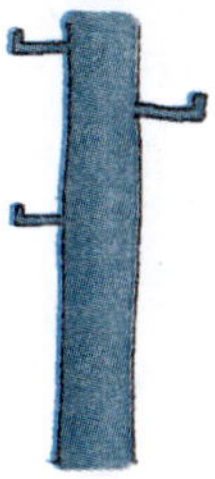

p __ l __

f __ x

h __ t

st __ n __

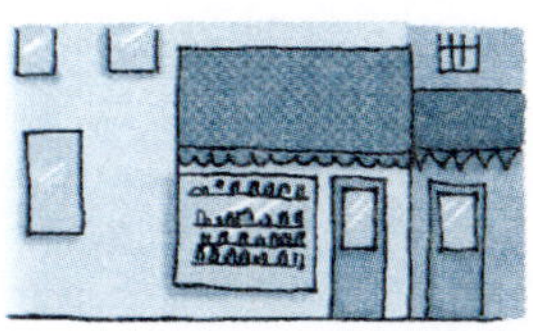

sh __ p

J __ __

Bud's Nap

Read the story and color each picture. Then circle the words in each sentence that have a long "e" sound, as in "me."

Bud's Nap

Bud sat under a big green tree. Bud was sleepy.

Three bees buzzed and the queen bee buzzed.

A bee sat on Bud's knee.

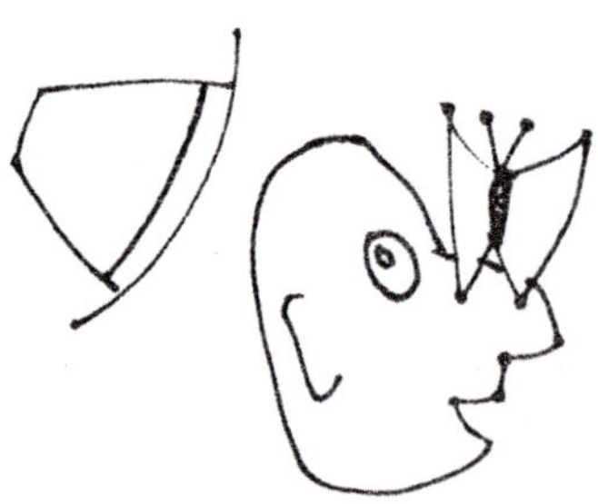

A butterfly sat on Bud's nose.

Bud jumped up. He did not feel sleepy anymore.

Complete each word with **"ee."** Then write and read the whole word.

b e e   bee

s__ __   s

gr__ __n   gr n

kn__ __   kn

sl__ __p   sl p

qu__ __n   qu n

Bud's Nap

Draw a line to connect the correct letters, then write the word.

sl — eep / im

sleep

b — ee / y

gr — een / eet

kn — it / ee

s — ea / ee

qu — ail / een

Find and color three pictures in a row with the same sound. Say the picture names.

short "e" sound, as in "bed."

long "e" sound, as in "sleep."

Bud's Nap

Read each sentence. Find the word that is wrong and write it in the red box. Write the correct word in the orange box.

Bud sat under a big grin tree.

The quick bee buzzed.

Bud did not sea the bees.

He did not fill sleepy anymore.

Make complete sentences using the words from the box.

was Bud asleep fast

☐☐☐ ☐☐☐ ☐☐☐☐

☐☐☐☐☐☐.

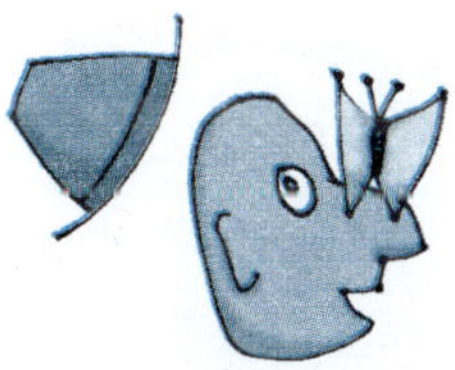

up woke Bud

☐☐☐ ☐☐☐☐ ☐☐!

more Bud snored

☐☐☐ ☐☐☐☐☐☐ ☐☐☐☐.

Bud's Nap

Read each sentence, then draw a line to the correct picture.

The bees saw Bud sitting under the tree.

Three bees buzzed and the queen bee buzzed.

A bee sat on Bud's hand.

The butterfly sat on Bud's nose.

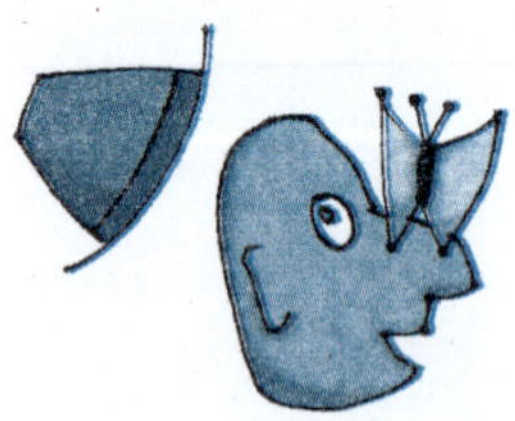

The butterfly flew into the sky.

Look at each picture and fill in the missing vowel for each word.

b _e_ d 

tr _e_ _e_ 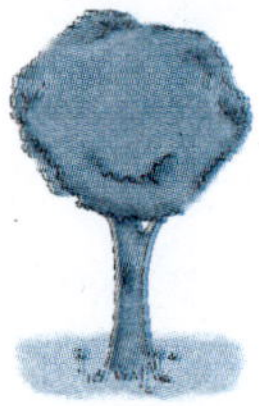

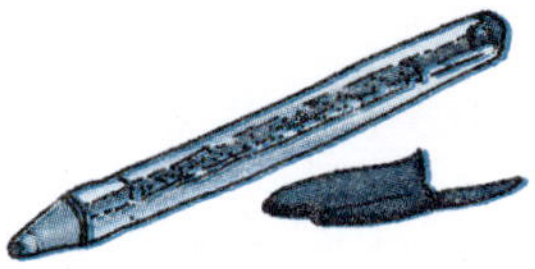

p __ n

b __ __

r __ d

gr __ __ n

thr __ __

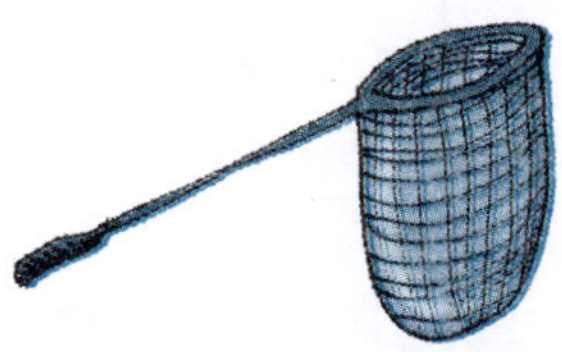

n __ t

The Picnic

Read the story and color each picture. Then circle the words in each sentence that have a long "e" sound, as in "eat."

The Picnic

Jill had hot dogs, buns, green peas, and beans.

She had meatballs and peanut butter.

She put the hot tea into a teapot.

She put the picnic in a basket.

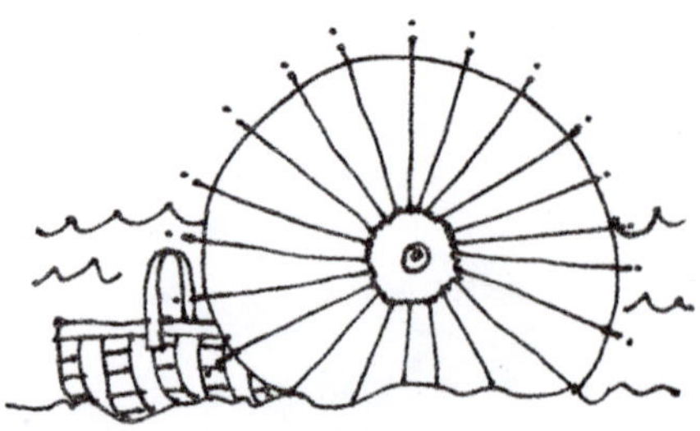

It was a treat to eat a picnic at the beach.

Complete each word with **"ea."** Then write and read the whole word.

b___ ___ch — b ch

b___ ___n — b n

p___ ___ch — p ch

f___ ___st — f st

cr___ ___m — cr m

t___ ___ — t

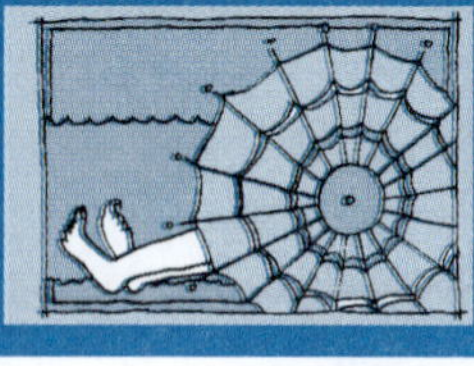

The Picnic

Draw a line to connect the correct letters.

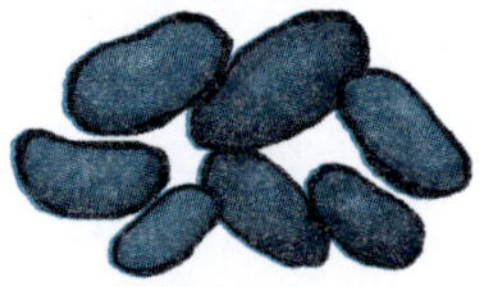

b ea l
s n

l ea ch
b sh

m ea t
f st

p ea ch
b st

t ea
f

tr ea t
cr m

Circle the word that goes with the picture, then write the word on the line.

bee
beach
left

bean
less
tea

beach
bean
peach

knee
feast
peach

cream
meet
shell

tree
feed
tea

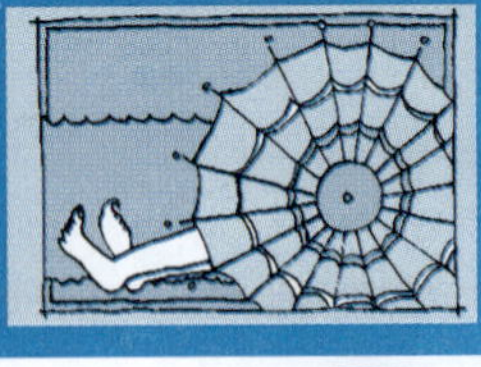

The Picnic

Read each sentence. Find the word that is wrong and write it in the red box. Write the correct word in the orange box.

Jill made hot tee.

It was time to eat the fist.

Jill went to the beech.

They sipped tea by the see.

Make complete sentences using the words from the box.

tea made Jill hot

.

by sat sea Tim

the .

went She beach

to the .

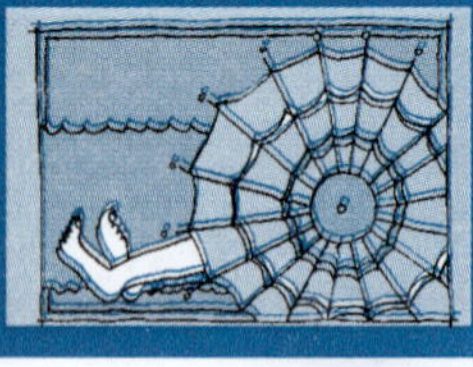

The Picnic

Read each sentence, then draw a line to the correct picture.

Jill fixed a big picnic.	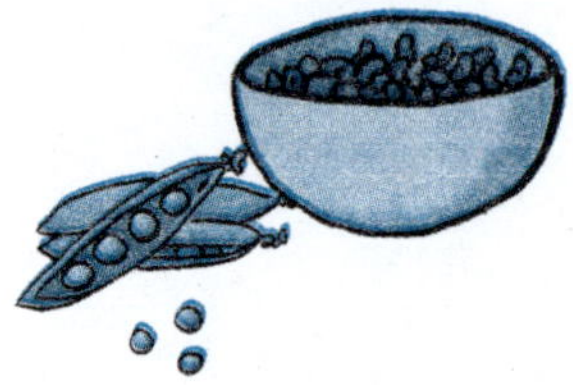
Jill had green peas and beans.	
Jill had meatballs and peanut butter.	
Jill put the hot tea into a teapot.	
It was a treat to swim in the chilly sea.	

Look at each picture and fill in the missing vowel for each word.

h e n 

l e a f 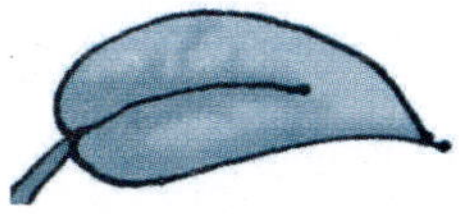

t ___ ___ pot

l ___ g

v ___ t

b ___ ___ n

b ___ ___ ch

m ___ n

The Train

Read the story and color each picture. Then circle the words in each sentence that have a long "a" sound, as in "main."

The Train

The little train was painted black.

The little train ran in the rain.

The cow just stood and looked and wagged her tail.

Soon a little maid came along with a shiny pail.

As the cow wagged her tail, the maid pumped milk into the pail.

Read and write the words.

tr	ai	n

train

p	ai	d

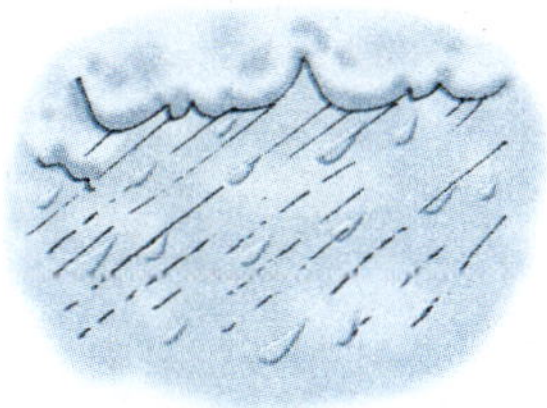

r	ai	n

p	ai	l

m	ai	d

t	ai	l

The Train

Draw a line to connect the correct letters.

p ai d

w i

m ai l

t n

br ai d

tr n

p ai n

r l

m ai d

s l

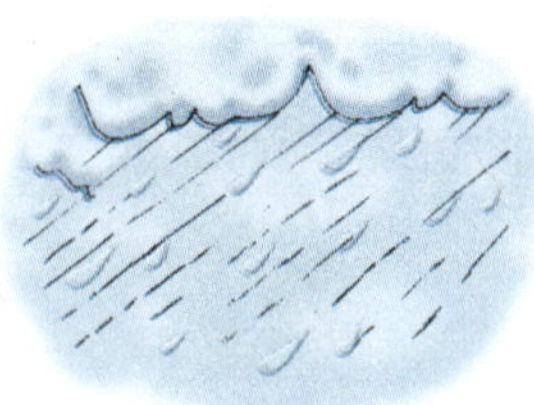

g ai n

r b

Unscramble the letters and write the word.
Draw a line to the correct picture.

n	tr	ai

train

ai	d	p

n	ai	r

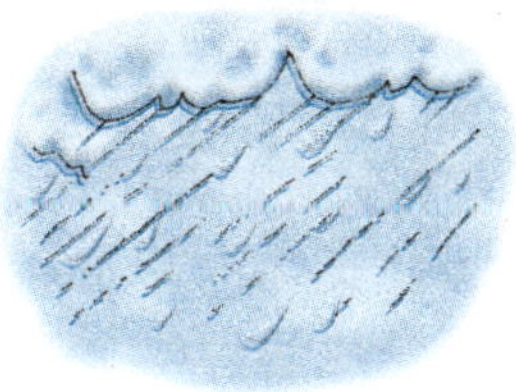

p	l	ai

ai	d	m

l	ai	t

The Train

Read each sentence. Find the word that is wrong and write it in the red box. Write the correct word in the orange box.

The little tray was painted black.

→

The little train ran in the pain.

→

The cow was not awake.

→

A little maid came along with a tail.

→

Write complete sentences using the words from the boxes.

ran	The little train	in the rain.

her tail.	wagged	The cow

ran	up the hill.	The train

The Train

Read each sentence, then draw a line to the correct picture.

The little train ran in the rain. ● ● 

It ran up the hill and down the hill. ● ● 

On the track was a big brown cow. ● ● 

A little maid came along with a shiny pail. ● ● 

The maid pumped milk into the pail. ● ● 

Look at each picture and color the correct vowel.

j a m

sn a i l

a

ai

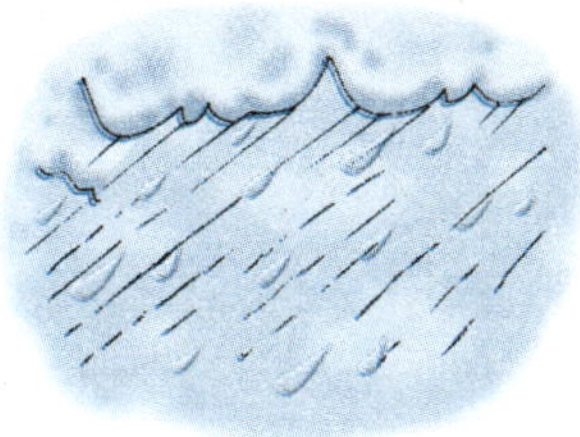

a

ai

a

ai

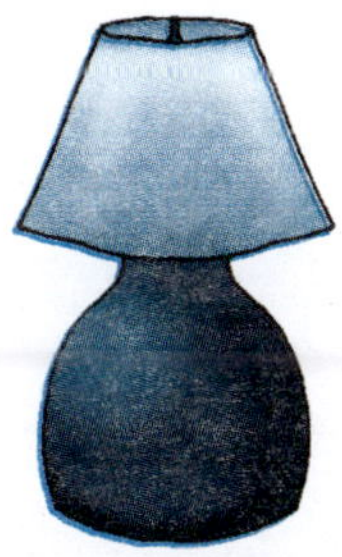

a

ai

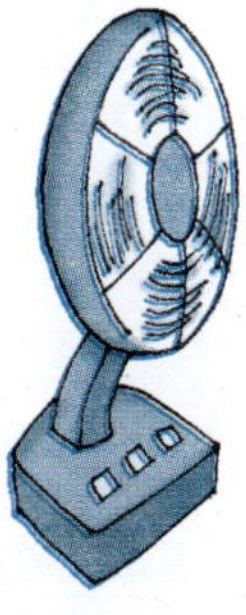

a

ai

a

ai

The Visit

Read the story and color each picture. Then circle the words in each sentence that have a long "o" sound, as in "bone."

The Visit

A mouse had a house in a stone wall.

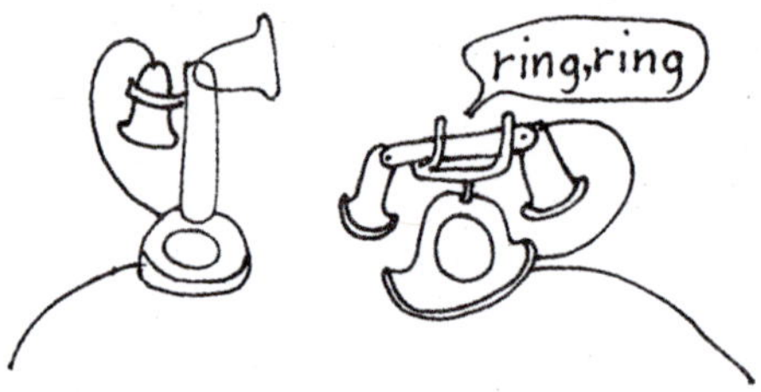

Mouse had a white phone. Toad had a red phone.

He put on his green coat and red slippers.

All the drivers were speeding past.

She took white paint and a big red card.

Read and write the words.

r o ck

tr u ck

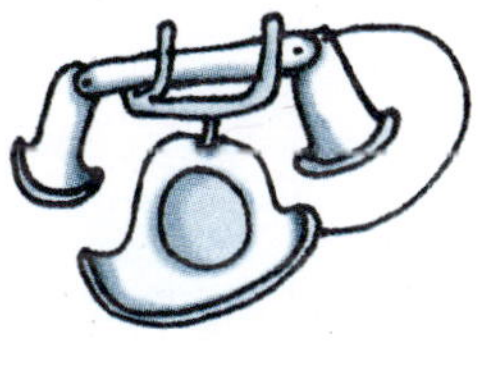

ph o n e

t oa d

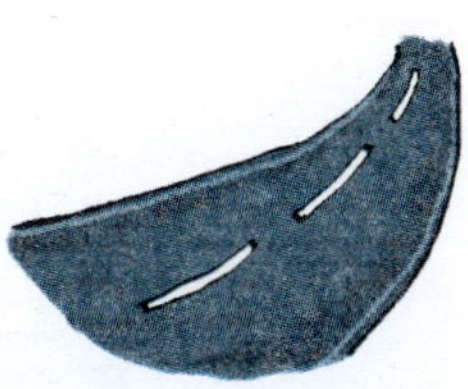

r oa d

c oa t

The Visit

Fill in the missing letters. Draw a line to the matching picture.

r _ c k 

t r _ c k 

p h _ n _ 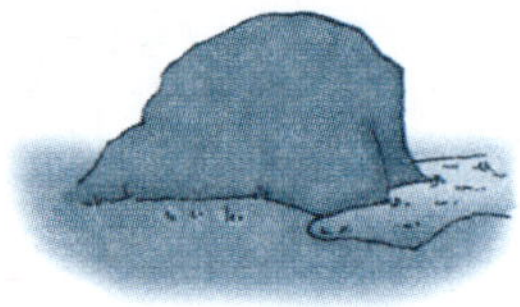

t _ _ d 

r _ _ d 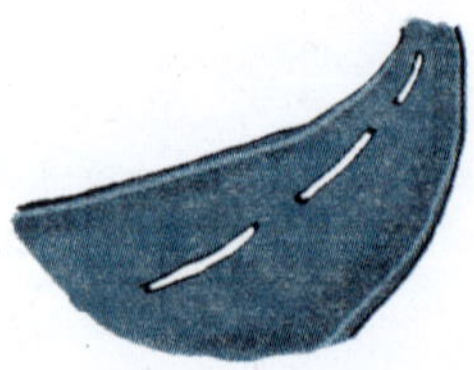

c _ _ t 

Find and color three pictures in a row with the same sound. Say the picture names.

long "o_e" sound, as in "home."

long "oa" sound, as in "road."

The Visit

Read each sentence. Find the word that is wrong and write it in the red box. Write the correct word in the orange box.

Mouse and goat are good pals.

Mouse had a white cone.

Toad put on his green boat.

Toad cannot get across the rod.

Write complete sentences using the words from the boxes.

had	Toad	a red phone.

his green coat.	put on	Toad

waved	Mouse	up and down.	the sign

The Visit

Read each sentence, then draw a line to the correct picture.

A mouse had a house in a stone wall. ●	● 
Toad had a red phone. ●	● 
All the drivers were speeding past. ●	● 
Toad sang a little tune. ●	● 
Toad put a tiny foot into the street. ●	● 

Look at each picture and color the correct vowel.

b <u>o</u> x 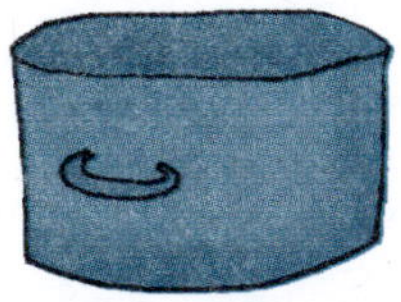

g <u>o</u> <u>a</u> t 

o
oa

o
oa

o
oa

o
oa

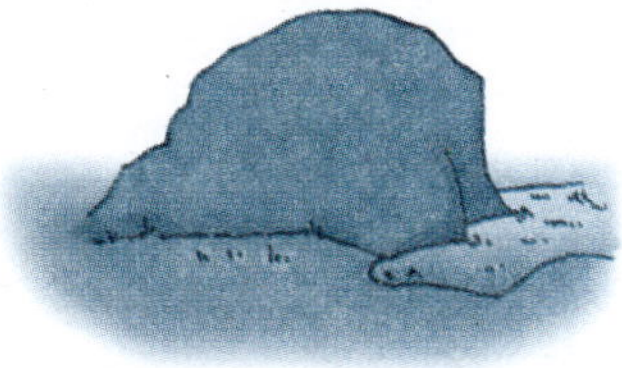

o
oa

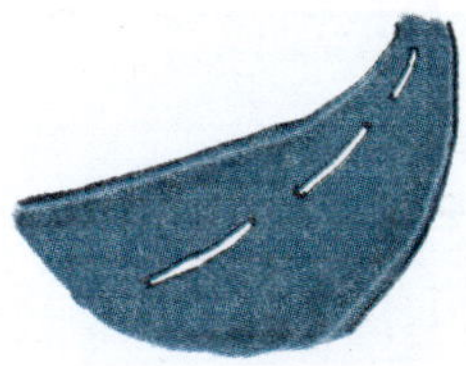

o
oa

Chickens

Read the story and color each picture. Then circle the words in each sentence that have a "cr," "ch," or "cl" sound, as in "crack," "chip," or "clap."

Chickens

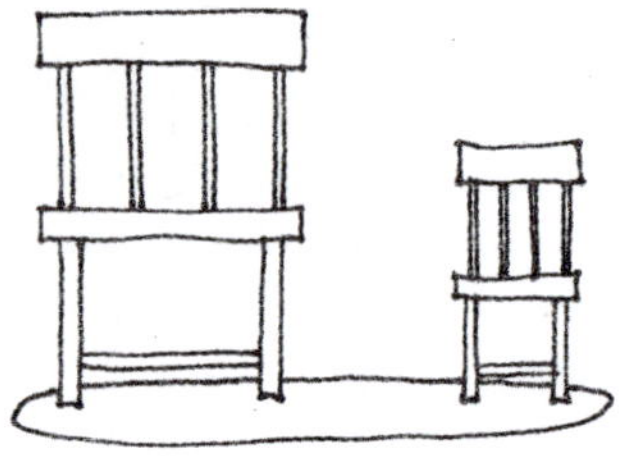

Chicken Big and Chicken Little had two chairs, a big chair and a little chair.

"Let us play a game," they said. "One, two, three, GO!"

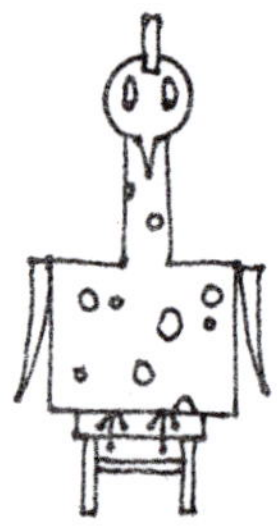

Chicken Big sat in the little chair.

Chicken Little cheered and clapped her wings.

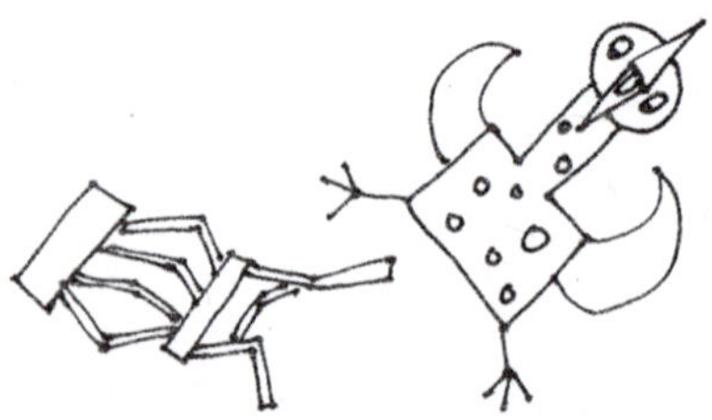

But all of a sudden, the little chair creaked, croaked, and broke!

Fill in the missing letters and write the words.

ai	ea	i	a	ee	a

ch ☐ se ____________________

ch ☐ r ____________________

cr ☐ sh ____________________

ch ☐ r ____________________

ch ☐ cken ____________________

cr ☐ k ____________________

Chickens

Draw a line to complete the word and fill in the missing letters.

cr | ch | air

c h air

cr | ch | ase

__ __ase

cr | ch | ash

__ __ash

cr | ch | icken

__ __icken

cr | ch | eer

__ __eer

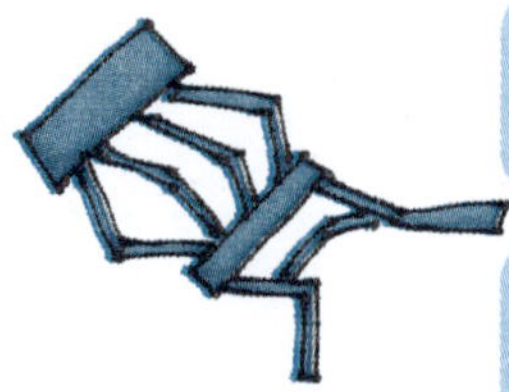

cr | ch | eak

__ __eak

Circle the word that goes with the picture, then write the word on the line.

chase
case
chain

chain
chair
care

cheer
cheap
chew

craim
crash
crack

chicken
child
chilly

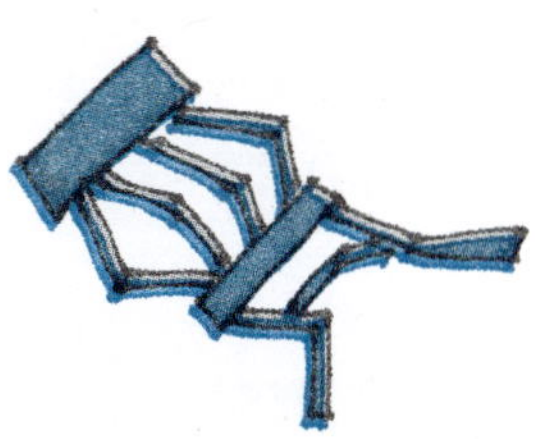

cream
creek
creak

Chickens

Read each sentence. Find the word that is wrong and write it in the red box. Write the correct word in the orange box.

Chicken Little sat in the big fair.

Let us say a game!

She nodded her heed.

Chicken Big chosed Chicken Little across the room.

Write complete sentences using the words from the boxes.

in the big chair.	Chicken Little	sat

clapped	her wings.	Chicken Big

her wings.	Chicken Big	checked

Chickens

Read each sentence, then draw a line to the correct picture.

Chicken Big chased Chicken Little across the room. ●

● 

Chicken Little sat in the big chair. ●

● 

Chicken Big cheered and clapped her wings. ●

● 

She nodded her head. ●

● 

Chicken Little ran to the big chair. ●

● 

Look at each picture and color the correct consonant blend.

cr o wn 

ch i n 

cr

ch

cr

ch

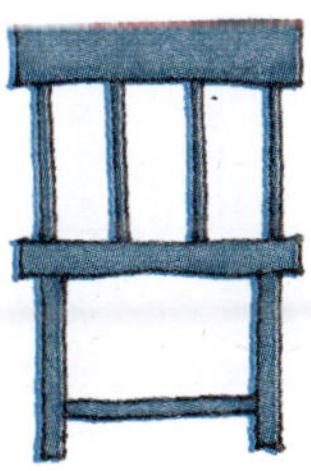

cr

ch

cr

ch

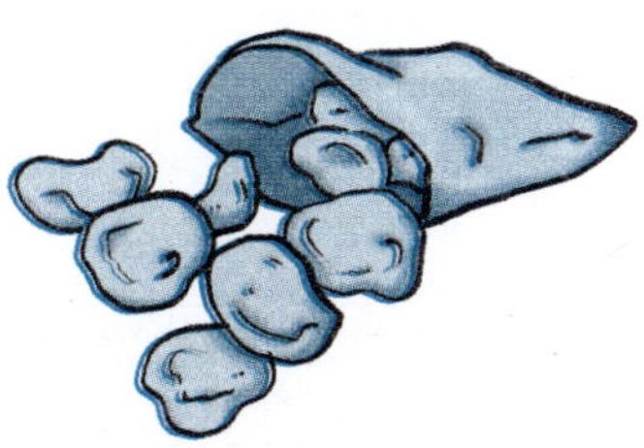

cr

ch

cr

ch

The King

Read the story and color each picture. Then circle the words in each sentence that have an "ng" sound, as in "sing."

The King

In the spring, the king sang a ringing song.

She did not smile. She did not like his song.

The king did not feel happy. He did not feel proud.

So the little girl went to see the king.

"Now at last we are friends," said the king with a grin.

Read and write the words.

b	a	ng

s	i	ng

k	i	ng

r	i	ng

wr	o	ng

str	o	ng

The King

Draw a line to complete the word and fill in the missing letters.

s — ing / eng

s__ __ __

b — ing / ang

b__ __ __

k — ang / ing

k__ __ __

r — ing / ong

r__ __ __

wr — ong / ung

wr__ __ __

str — ong / ing

str__ __ __

Unscramble the letters and write the word.
Draw a line to the correct picture.

i	s	ng

wr	ng	o

ng	r	i

a	ng	b

i	k	ng

ng	o	str

The King

Read each sentence. Find the word that is wrong and write it in the red box. Write the correct word in the orange box.

She did not like his long.

The sing did not feel happy.

The bell did bring.

He spoke in a tone very string.

Write complete sentences using the words from the boxes.

in the spring. | was | The king | happy

sang | the song. | The girl

her foot. | She | stamped

The King

Read each sentence, then draw a line to the correct picture.

The little girl went to see the king. ● ● 

The king sang a ringing song. ● ● 

The king was happy in the spring. ● ● 

The girl frowned and stamped her foot. ● ● 

The king went to bed. ● ● 

Look at each picture and color the correct blends.

ang

ing

ong

ang

ing

ong

ang

ing

ong

ang

ing

ong

ang

ing

ong

ang

ing

ong

colour the little fairy with wings.

How many dogs can you spot?

Follow the pattern and draw what comes next in the empty box.

Count the number of buses, helicopters and ships.

BOB
BOOKS
SET 2
Advancing Beginners

STAGE 2: DEVELOPING READER
BOB
BOOKS
SET 3
Word Families

STAGE 1: STARTING TO READ
BOB
BOOKS
SET 1

BOB
BOOKS

STAGE 1: STARTING TO READ
BOB
BOOKS
More
Beginning Readers

BOB
BOOKS
SET 4
Complex Words

BOB
BOOKS
SET 5
Long Vowels